ANTHOLOGY OF POETRY
BY
YOUNG AMERICANS®

1996 EDITION
VOLUME CII

Published by Anthology of Poetry, Inc.

©*Anthology of Poetry by Young Americans*®
1996 Edition
Volume CII

Printed in the United States of America

To submit poems
for consideration in the 1997 edition of the
Anthology of Poetry by Young Americans®,
send to:

> Anthology of Poetry, Inc.
> PO Box 698
> Asheboro, NC 27204-0698

Authors responsible
for originality of poems submitted.

The Anthology of Poetry, Inc.
307 East Salisbury • P.O. Box 698
Asheboro, NC   27204-0698

ISBN: 1-883931-05-3

Anthology of Poetry by Young Americans®
is a registered trademark of
Anthology of Poetry, Inc.

We have had another wonderful year editing the 1996 edition of the <u>Anthology of Poetry by Young Americans</u>®. After seven years the poems are still as fresh and original as our first edition. Our belief that children live and think in poetic images is again confirmed by the poetry of this edition. If you want to know what is on the minds of our children, poetry is the window. This edition will let you look through that window to a world prose could never describe. To a world painted with wonder, awe and sometimes confusion, with microscopic inspection of subjects that adults hardy notice and with insight into issues adults also struggle with. We tried to present the poems as the author wrote them, in their format and punctuation. We would like to extend a special thanks to all the poets who participated. We are expecting great things from them in the future.

The Editors

AS THE YEARS GO BY

As the years go by
I know my grandma has wings to fly
She's been an angel I know that has to be
She's high above now she's wild and free
But how can that be I think it's God
He gives her the power
of a flower.

As the years go by
More and more I wish I could fly
I would go fly so high I would reach the sky
If I could fly I would go see my grandma and say hi
The bad thing would be I wouldn't want to say bye.

As the years go by
I wish I would've had a chance to say good-bye
She was lying in the bed eating food
from a tube.

As the years go by
I think of her and where she would lie
And all the things she would buy.
Almost all the time she was funny telling jokes
to a lot of folks.

As the years go by
I wish she wouldn't have gone away
But all we could do was pray.

Vanessa Garcia
Age: 11

PRETTY BLUE SKY

The sky is so blue,
very pretty,
and looks so bright and new.
When it comes night,
the blue sky is gone.
But wait until morning,
and it appears once again.

On sad days it's raining,
on fun days it's not.
I wish I can go up,
very high in the sky,
and when I come back,
I'll tell you no lies,
that I love, I love the
pretty blue sky.

Tiffany Green
Age: 13

LAUGHING CLOUD

Living in the forest, trying to cook.
Laughing Cloud, the legoo,
Came to my house and all the children cry "look!"
She tells us many stories,
She stays 'til morning.

Brandy Simpson
Age: 8

C hristmas
H appy things
R eindeer
I mpossible things
S now
T otally cool gifts
M erry time of year
A miracle
S anta

Steve Boardwine
Age: 11

I have a cat
Who is very very fat
His favorite thing is to eat
Turkey is his favorite meat
Ditto is the name of the cat
Oh, did I mention he is fat
Once we gave him a turkey treat
He ate it in a heartbeat
Some think he is crazy
Me, I think he's just flat lazy
The color of the cat is bright
It's orange, of course. Oh, what a sight
Well, that's it about my cat
Who likes to sleep in a hat

Lindsay Mongenas

POEMS

There are many types of poems.

Happy poems.
Sad poems.
Scary poems.
Silly poems.
Rhyming poems.
Long poems.
Short poems.
Holiday poems.

Sarah Young
Age: 10

MONEY OF THE SEA

Just because I'm a sand dollar
   doesn't mean I'm made of sand.
I just bury myself in the sand all day;
   it's so much fun.
And when all the laughing and playing is done,
   up to the top of the ocean I'll go.
Until the current comes along,
   I'll flow in the water like a breeze or a song.
      Bye,
         it's time to fly,
            right through the sea.

Sarah Calugar
Age: 10

ON MY WAY TO CHURCH
(A PILGRIM POEM)

On my way to church one day,
To me and to my group's dismay,
A giant bobcat jumped out of the wood.
I tried to do something, but no one could.
One girl fainted, a girl named Kay.

We yelled and yelled and yelled for help,
But nothing came, not even Kelp.
Not a thing could save us from this.
"Our rifles!" shouted a guy named Chris.
"DON'T DO THAT!" we heard someone faraway yelp.

Then it came into sight.
The Grand High Bobcat of Mightiest Might!
"He is my son, don't kill him."
Then, he proclaimed, "Get over here, Kim!"
Then, the dad said, "Hold on tight!"

They were gone like that,
Those dangerous cats.
We went on to church the rest of the way.
And when we got there, we shouted, "HOORAY!"
"I can't believe we survived," cried a guy named Pat.

George L. Seibel, IV
Age: 10

5

THE FLYING SQUIRREL

While sitting in my tree house,
On a very lonely day,
I gazed out of the window,
A little squirrel walked in my way.

A cocky little fellow,
He walked across my window proud,
Leaped onto my shoulder,
And chortled something loud.

"When you're flying," he yapped,
"Please take my advice,
Keep your head up high,
And never look down twice.

Otherwise you'll fall,
And fall fast until,
Your stomach will drop,
Into the ground you'll drill."

"How would you know?,"
I replied in a smart aleck way.
The squirrel turned its nose,
Grew wings and flew away.

Meredith Irwin
Age: 12

6

RIDING A BIKE IN THE WOODS

Some days on my bike,
I ride to the park
To go on the trails.

I glide and coast
Down the steep trail,
Bouncing and trying to stay on the path.

I try to avoid
Trees, rocks and other obstacles,
While squeezing my brakes ever so tightly.

Wind blows through my hair,
Leaves and mud everywhere,
It's such a great feeling to be here!

To the bottom I go!
Having had a great time,
Looking around and getting my bearing.

I then discover,
As every time before,
That going up is not quite as much fun.

Brad Pace
Age: 12

CHRISTMAS MYSTERY

One cold and snowy night,
A dark figure came into sight.

It was on my roof,
With black snowy hooves.

It was brown and hairy,
Friendly, not scary.

I looked out my window only to see,
The strange creature staring at me.

I shrieked in fright,
And ran out of sight.

Then the animal started to glow,
For what reason I do not know.

I think I've heard of this creature years before,
Now it was practically knocking at my door.

Ah, yes, I remember now!

The reason for its incredible glow,
It's for leading Santa through the snow.

Santa? Santa? Who is this fellow?
Does he wear pink, green, red, or yellow?

Red, I think, is what he wears,
He comes down the chimney, not down the stairs.

He certainly is one for the holidays,
And when you're nice, it really pays.

Presents and toys,
For good girls and boys.

But is he real?
I mean, what's the deal?

Was this all just a dream?
What does this all mean?

It means Christmas is finally here!!!

Marian McGavran
Age: 12

PANDAS

Pandas are black and white,
But do not forget their might.
Pandas may not be very slow,
But they take their time in snow.
Pandas eat a lot of bamboo
So that is what they feed them at the zoo.
Pandas may get extinct,
If we don't do something distinct.

Jessica Feghali
Age: 12

A SOLDIER'S HEART

In the winter's bitterness,
Of 1944,
The greatest heart was dying.

Taken by chance,
To a forsaken land,
Where he spent many nights dreaming.

Marched through red flares,
For over a year,
His heart was burnt and indented with fear.

Then finally the stripes had come,
To discover a dead heart,
Lying in dried blood.

So many awful memories,
and physical wounds,
Engraved into a heart forever gone.

Ward Stern
Age: 14

DADDY

I love my daddy.
I love my daddy so.
I miss him all the time.
I cry when he has to go.

Caitlin Lux

DARKENED LAND

Day is out, night is asleep,
Not hours 'til the night will creep.

The sun dies down, and the night picks up day,
Now the night will throw day away.

A robe of darkness covers the land,
Now the stars and night go hand in hand.

The land is pitch black except for one light,
It's the light of the moonbeam staring at a sight.

The sight is a sun ray peering in the sky,
That means night is over, oh, what a sigh.

But we must not fear, for night will reappear,
A time in a darkened land.

Mindi Naticchioni
Age: 11

MY DAY IN THE COUNTRY

Woke up in my cabin
My feet were cold
I never noticed I needed,
a new stove.
I started a fire
Then went outside to
look at the sky
The plains and mountains ahead
I saw a bird it was red
I looked at the tree, its
bark and leaves.
I went over to the tree
I felt as though I was three
Because it was so tall
I started to climb it.
It started to sway
I started to fall
When I landed I fell on leaves.
I felt as though I had fleas.
When I went inside
I started to cry.
When I went to bed
I hit my head.
I was happy to be OK!!

Marian Johnson
Age: 11

LEAVES

Leaves fall down
Leaves hit the ground
Leaves cover the ground like a blanket of snow
Then you have to rake them in a nice straight row
Next you rake them in a pile
With a great big smile
Then you put them in a big black bag
Around that big black bag you wrap a little tag
So the leaves don't fall out
And fly about
Now you are done
And so is the fun

R. J. Niemer
Age: 11

HATE

Why hate? Not everyone has it.
Or do they? Hate is an over-rated
thing. It's not as bad as people
make it. Black, white it's all right,
we're all the same right? So why
fight? Stop the hate!
Start the peace!

Ben Herche
Age: 13

HALLOWEEN SURPRISE

My friends and I are going trick-or-treating.
But I'm still at the table eating.
I stood up and said oh no!
Aren't you going to wait for me.
In my yard by the old hickory tree.
As we were going down the street.
There was something at my feet.
I couldn't tell what it was.
But I think it was some fuzz.
I kept on finding more and more.
Soon it led me to a door.
I turned and said, "Come on guys"
As the little old lady handed me a prize.
All my friends said, "Hurry and open it up!"
Out jumped a furry little pup!
That explains all the fuzz on the walk.
But we better get back because it's 11:00!

Beth Fleckenstein

BASKETBALL

Basketball is neat,
because I got new shoes for my feet.
We're going to have a good team,
by doing a lot of schemes.
It's going to be fun,
because we don't have to run.
It's going to be cool,
because we got an awesome school.

Jimmy Jauch
Age: 11

BASKETBALL

Basketball is a sport with just
Shoes, a shirt, and shorts.

With only ten seconds to go,
Boy I hate that guy in the third row.

I have only one try to make my wish
Then all of the sudden - SWISH!!

On pours the media, I don't know what to say
I don't do it on purpose,
That's just how I play.

Joey Schmidt
Age: 11

BIRD IN A TREE

I see a bird up in a tree,
I think he's going to peck at me.
If that birdie pecks at me,
I'll shoot him right down from that tree.
When that bird falls to the ground,
I'll bury him in a dirt mound.
When he's gone I will not moan,
Nor will I buy him a gravestone.
I will sit back in delight,
Who cares if I did wrong or right.

Brian Wissel
Age: 11

NIAGARA FALLS

The water crashes and sounds like thunder;
It made me stand and stare in wonder.

We saw the falls from far and near;
we went below and saw them from the rear.

The falls are quite an amazing sight;
a real display of force and might.

Niagara Falls is a spectacular place to see;
just for me.

Gus Albers
Age: 13

OLD SAM

Poor old Sam,
All he does is make jam!
He is so very poor,
I wish I could give him more.
His favorite thing to do,
Is make jam that's red, purple and blue!
He loves all the kids,
So he lets them lick his jelly lids.
When he was on his bed about to die,
All the children stood around him
and said, "Good-bye!"

Katie Vale
Age: 11

CANDY

Candy is so sweet
And so good to eat
Sometimes I skip lunch
Just so I can munch
My mother gets mad
And so does my dad
But I tell them to go away
So I can eat my Milky Way

Rachel Agnew
Age: 11

A SOCCER GAME

If she will score,
I will shoot two more.
I look up and see,
Two girls coming at me,
Should I yield?
As I dribble down the field,
For when the whistle is blown,
Who will groan?
If they have won,
I will still know I had fun.

Anne Quinn
Age: 11

HALLOWEEN NIGHT

Please don't scare me,
Please don't scare me,
Guess you don't know what day it is,
It's HALLOWEEN NIGHT.
I'm so scared that I'm going to scream,
And then all of a sudden,
I heard leaves rustling and then . . . . .
AAH! AAH! AAH! AAH!
A big furry monster popped out.
Fooled ya, it's just my mom.

Erinn Young

THE RAIN IS FALLING DOWN

Rain, rain falling down,
Dripping, dripping all around,
Tapping at my window,
Knocking on the door,
Dripping from the rooftops,
Falling to its floor.
Sometimes slowly
Sometimes fast
Sometimes loudly
Then - it stops - at last.

Amy Namaky
Age: 11

SCARY NIGHT

One Halloween night everyone
was in a fright
But there's no one in sight
then four things I felt bite

Oh my! A black cat
Oh no! A fat bat
Oh! A hairy rate
Oh my! A vampire named Pat
This is one scary night!

Ryan Lynn
Age: 11

STEADY BEAT

I walk down the street
to a steady beat.
A leaf falls "crash."
I stepped on one "smash."
There's a puddle in the road,
And look there's a toad.
All these things I see
They make me feel happy.

Derek J. Scott
Age: 12

TREES

Trees stand so big and tall
When I stand next to one
I feel very small

Their leaves are colors of
Red, orange, and green
They're scattered all over
Making a beautiful scene

Their branches are all shapes and sizes
The new seasons come
and bring new surprises.

Maria Trotta
Age: 11

HALLOWEEN NIGHT

On Halloween night
the goblins are in sight.
As the sun disappears
the witches come near.

The bats come out
making screechy shouts.
And the ghosts that fly
are high in the sky.

Pumpkins are carved with different faces,
children having lots of races.
Children dressed in different colors,
"Have fun," say all their mothers.

Houses are decorated with scary things,
children are scared as the doorbell rings.
Trick-or-treat, trick-or-treat,
all the goblins speak.

As their bags get full
of sweet things to eat.

Nicole Bessler
Age: 11

WATERFALLS

Waterfalls
Streaming waterfalls
Silently trickling downstream
Peacefully falling

Janet Nester
Age: 12

AFTER SCHOOL

Every day when I get home.
I open the door, ohh there's the phone.
It must be a quarter 'til three,
My friends surely know it's me,
Because I am the only one.
But Mom says, "Not until homework's done!"
Do I listen? I sure try but I always ask her why?
I love the excitement and the fun,
I try to listen to everyone!
Sometimes it's hard to concentrate,
But maybe, MAYBE, Mom will be late.
Then I will have more time to talk.
Maybe I can even take the dog on a walk.
Turn off the radio, clean my mess,
Sometimes a kid has a lot of stress.
Because Moms and Dads don't understand,
That all that homework hurts your hand!

Angela Lay
Age: 12

DOGS

Dogs, dogs, dogs,
Rough, funny, silly dogs
Spotted, black, furry dogs

Amy Dangel
Age: 12

A MAGICAL BLANKET

A fairyland - that's what it was
Twinkling, shining
White, magical dust
Sprinkled everywhere

Icicles shimmered in the bright
Sunshine
So delicate, so fragile
Nothing could destroy this beautiful
Blanket of snow
Not a sound anywhere

Nothing but a soft breeze
Suddenly I saw it
One tiny snowflake drifting down...
Landing...
To complete this beautiful, magical,
Snow-white blanket.

Christina Grothaus
Age: 12

The mountains I see are usually pretty,
They are majestic and magic and very fantastic,
Sometimes purple, violet or blue,
When I see them I think of you,
When it's time to say good-bye,
I'm about to cry,
The mountains I see are usually pretty.

Jenni Gettler
Age: 9

BUMBLEBEE

See that yellow bumblebee.
I think he's flying after me.
If he stings me I will shout.
Ouch. . .
Will you pull the stinger out?

Michael Murphy
Age: 11

BASEBALL

An American pastime, baseball
The crack of the bat, the roar of the crowd
  Those are fine and well
But best of all the food, the hotdogs, pizza,
popcorn, candy and pop
  For that is what makes the game great

Mike Schachleiter
Age: 11

HALLOWEEN

There is a night called Halloween.
All the ghosts, goblins and witches come out to haunt.
You go door-to-door for candy.
You say "trick-or-treat."
But be careful of what you eat.

Ashley Schmidt
Age: 11

LIFE

Life is of the world and the things that breathe,
It is of men and of the plants which heath.
Life is of nature's beautiful citation,
Which makes the earth a natural sensation.
Life is of you; Life is of me.
Life is wonderful, we all will agree.
Life is a time that is precious to all,
Life is the time that we should have a ball.
It is the torch with the brightest flame.
We all play our part as if in a game.
Life is to have, life is to use.
Life is something not to abuse.
Life is the warmth under your skin.
Life is the time when you're sure to sin.
One day your life will certainly fall,
So life is truly the best time of all.

Dustin Davis
Age: 13

Football
mean, tough
tackling, throwing, blitzing
it is pure work
Football

Nicholas Niemeier
Age: 9

ONCE UPON A TIME

Once upon a time, a goose drank wine,
a monkey swung on a sweet potato vine,
the vine broke, the monkey choked,
and they all went to Heaven on a billy goat.

Half way there they said
"Why don't we go to the other side"
So they turned around and then
they went to the other.
And half way there they said
"Why don't we go to the other side"

So they turned around, and went
to the other side.
And they went to Heaven and they
stayed in Heaven forever and ever.

Julia Finn
Age: 8

"Mommy, Daddy, take me to SEVEN ELEVEN."
"Why son?"
'Cause I really think it's heaven,
SEVEN ELEVEN.
It's really, really heaven.
'Cause it's SEVEN ELEVEN!'

Matthew Clifton
Age: 8

A CHILLY NIGHT IN PHOENIX

It's a cool night in a quiet town,
But the characteristics are upside-down,
  For in Sun Devil Stadium the Cowboys will play
The Jacksonville Jaguars, their waiting prey.
  This game is the top,
This game is the end,
  The officials tonight
Are nobody's friends
  "Hello, ladies and gentlemen,"
The announcer announces.
  "As always, drinks are fifty cents,
per twelve ounces.
  Game programs tonight are never a bore,
They're available for two dollars at the main door."
  The coin is flipped, the Cowboys win.
Dallas fans are shouting up a din.
  For fans' information, the Cowboys are favored,
The exact line, however, has been updated and wavered.
  The first guess was forty, but then, oh dear me,
The final line was estimated as ninety-three!
  Oh, so powerful,
The Cowboys won't yield,
  They elect to receive,
They run onto the field.
  The kick is long ,
But not long enough.
  As the Jag's will soon see,
The Cowboys are tough.
  To the forty, the fifty,
The Cowboys will run,
  They'll finally be stopped
At the Jag's forty-one.

The teams line up,
The signal, the snap,
    A reasonable run,
The fans will clap.
    It's second and one,
The play is mapped,
    But very strangely,
The 'Boys Q.B. is sacked!
    It actually happened,
Very ironically,
    A fantastic defensive play,
Perhaps symbolically.
    A symbol on second and one,
Maybe it's what the experts expected.
    For on the very next play,
The ball was intercepted!
    Quite a stunning play,
The Jag's players will dash
    And the score is six
To zip like a flash!
    The extra point is blocked,
Certainly not ashame.
    A whole lot of fans
Want the Cowboys to reign.
    I would tell the rest,
And the rest I will send,
    But for the reader's benefit,
I'll go straight to the end.
    Somehow by chance,
When their bright uniforms got dirty,
    The Cowboys limped,
To a score of thirty-five to thirty.
    With two seconds left,
The Jag's would have one more chance,

To prove their tiny worth
Before they got to wash their pants.
　With the Jag's behind by five,
Everyone could see,
　That the score wasn't up
Where they thought it would be.
　The Jacksonville dream
Had come to at last,
　But just might not make it
If they can't catch the pass.
　The Jacksonville quarterback
Lines up and throws,
　He misses the receiver,
But a Dallas Cowboy hits him in the nose!
　The ref calls interference
On the defense, number 43
　The penalty was in the end zone, touchdown!
And the Jaguars quarterback will be the M.V.P.

Daniel Schwallie

CARS

Sometimes I love cars
because they take me places.
Sometimes I hate them
because they don't have to tie shoe laces.

Maxwell Holt
Age: 8

MY PUPPY BARNEY

I thought my puppy Barney
was such a cute little pup
until I woke-up this morning,
he went on the living room rug!
I shook my finger at him
and boy, that made him cry,
but that never did stop him
from eating my whole apple pie.
He tipped over the garbage,
and boy, that made me steam!
He also pushed over the bookshelf,
and I really wanted to scream!
I just fell over
because this is too extreme!

Caitlin Cronin
Age: 9

TIME HEALS A BROKEN HEART

It's a painful thing, when a loved one dies.
    Whenever they're mentioned someone cries.
It's like your heart breaks in half,
    when your loved one starts a new path.
I know how you feel, I've been there, too,
        but after time you won't feel so blue.

Christine Marie Benken
Age: 13

FRIENDS

Friends are like summer,
ice cream cones melting and freezing.
Friends are like fall,
leaves falling and rising in the wind.
Friends are like winter,
shining, sparkling your life like snow.
Friends are like spring,
flowers growing and losing petals in the wind.
Friends are like seasons,
always changing, coming and going.

Anna Nolan

CHRISTMAS NIGHT

The star was so bright,
People watched it in the night
Watching all the scenes of
the shepherd kings.
Walking toward the light
that was so bright
It was such a beautiful sight to see,
a little baby lying in the night.

Angela Murphy
Age: 12

FRIENDS

Friends are very thoughtful,
in many special ways.
They help you with your homework,
and invite you over to play.

They talk with you at recess,
and play all kinds of games.
They're truthful and kind,
and never call you names.

Friends are very nice to have,
especially when you're down.
They make you feel real special,
I think I'll keep a few around.

Elisa Perin

FOOTBALL

Football, football you're so cool!
Because you have a Super Bowl
When the runner runs the ball
The ref blows the whistle to call his call.
I like you football very much
Because you have a special touch.

David Lorentz
Age: 9

DREAMS...

Some dreams are happy
And some dreams are sad.
Some dreams are good
And some dreams are bad.
Dreams can be wonderful,
They fill me with delight.
But dreams can be terrible,
They can also bring fright.
I hope you have nice dreams,
And the good ones come true.
It will make the bad ones
Easier to get through.

Tricia Klonne
Age: 10

I WISH

I wish I had a kitten,
With little purple mittens,
And a little pink bow-tie,
Except Mom says "No,
You already have a puppy,"
So I guess I won't get a kitten
until I grow up, but
Wouldn't that be great!

Lindsey Ehlers
Age: 9

RUNNING

Running running down the street,
Who is going to be the first one to get the meat?
Running running faster faster
Still want to win front row seats?

Emily Mustard
Age: 9

WISHES

I wish I had a cat with long black hair.
I wish I had a dog to walk and care.
I wish I had a lot of money in my pocket
so I could buy a pretty new locket.

Amy Brinkman

TOURNAMENT GAME '95

The clouds are gray
It's time to play
Because soccer never waits

For four quarters
We ran and ran passed and passed
And took our best shots

Our opponents did the same
So at the end of the game
The score was aught to aught

Overtime came
And so did the rain
But the score stayed the same

To shoot-outs we go
And with this we know
Someone would win this game

To our disappointment
We did not win
But we left the field with a grin

"Because we played our best game of the year"

Stephanie Norton
Age: 10

A DOG IN A LOVING HOME

Dogs are man's best friend,
They always wait for you to come around the bend,
Dogs are always willing to defend,
Your home illnesses he or she will mend.

Dogs will not rely,
On Thanksgiving and the pumpkin pie,
But only on the love you share,
That you give them here and there,

And to this day dogs still are,
A special part of our hearts.

Delia Michael

HOSSY BOY OUR DOG

Hossy Boy is our dog.
He is a big fat hog.
He has a room.
Where there is a broom.
He eats our food right off the table.
He would do it every day if he were able.
But even though, we love him so !!!!!!!!

Elise Mitchell
Age: 9

THE RAIN JUST KEEPS ON FALLING

The rain just keeps on falling and
the sky is colored gray
the birds don't stop their singing
because it's just another day and
the clouds keep passing over
bringing rain to flowers and
it's just a golden glow.

Charles Lee Johnson, III
Age: 12

FANTASY

One day I had a dream
Along a little stream
That I could fly.
I flew across lands far and near
I saw pyramids, grass so green
Desert sands, and oceans blue
But when I got back who was there, who?
No one but me
The little stream
And the memory of my dream.

Kristene Templeton
Age: 12

FALL LEAVES

Orange: the aged color gives warmth

Yellow: the brightness gives beauty

Brown: the chocolate shade tells me
         how special the season is:

    F antastic colors
    A lways warm
    L ovely
    L ively

Sarah Elizabeth Purtell
Age: 11

MY DADDY GAVE ME A LION

My daddy gave me a lion,
I really shouldn't be cry'n.
For my daddy didn't die,
so why am I so shy?
My mom came to my room one day,
to tell me that I should not stay.
I told her that I wouldn't go,
downstairs to see a TV show.

Andrea Bouldin
Age: 9

GRANDMAS

Grandmas are there when you're blue
They know what you're thinking when
no one else has a clue.
Grandmas are wise
and have been around for awhile.
If you need something, just give them a dial.
Grandmas are smart
They know what's best.
Grandmas can do anything
Just put them to the test.
Grandmas are there through thick-and-thin.
They're your friend 'til the end.

Matthew Eric Bradshaw
Age: 10

MY MOTHER GAVE ME A KANGAROO!

My mother gave me a Kangaroo!
It hopped right in the kitchen stew.
It took my mother's dressing shoe!
It put them on,
hopped downstairs,
saw my mom.
She said, "You're going back today!"

Brittany Brownfield
Age: 8

IF

If I were a puppy,
And you were a dog,
Would you not talk with me,
Because I play like a hog?

If I were a slug,
And you were a bug,
Would you not say hi,
Because I love to tug?

If I was a bulb,
And you were a light,
Would you not join,
To light up the night?

So cooperate with each other,
And don't argue unless,
You want to be alone,
By not being your best.

Jenetta Marvene Thomas
Age: 11

I HATE

Everyone I know hates
Schools,
Especially all those
Dumb rules,

Another thing I really
Hate,
While I'm fishing I run
Out of bait,

I hate it when the radio
Becomes erratic,
But when it's clear I
Become ecstatic,

I don't like to eat many
Greens,
Especially all those lima
Beans.

Shauntel Nicole Stripling
Age: 11

MY PLACE

my place up high no one can see.
i sit and read, i sit and think, sometimes i sit and
laugh, or cry, sometimes i pray.
my place is up high comfortable and cozy
no one notices me in the trees.

Jessica Vickery
Age: 12

CHAMPIONS AND LOSERS

The game was ended,
One team victorious
The other overthrown.

One team celebrating,
The other in gloom.
The final basket decided it all.

One team slapping fives,
The other team shedding tears
With no more fears of losing.

But like most seasons,
As usual they end in a loss,
Except for the champions.

Ian F. Kinsley
Age: 14

THE UNHAPPY SOUL

Sara Smith was as woman of mystery,
For she would never share her past history,
The quiet people of the town,
They looked at her mop and frown,
And the frown was from sole to crown,

For she was the unhappiest soul around,
And she would never look up, she always looked down,
There were noises in her head,
And they found her in her bed,
She was lying there cold and dead.

Simone Monet-Williams

BASKETBALL

Basketball is a fun sport,
You can be either tall or short.
It is pretty easy to play,
You can play it on any day.
You can play it when it's hot,
You can play it when it's not.
There are many great players who played the game,
All of them think the same.
They think the NBA is the best,
Put the competition to rest.

Jonathan Katerberg
Age: 13

MY MESSY ROOM

Honey, your room is a mess!
On the floor you have my new dress!
Now baby, just look at your clock!
On top of it is your old sock!
Your drawers have shoes inside them,
I know you were trying to hide them.
Your books have torn out pages.
They haven't been read in ages!
Your twenty dollar calendar is on the floor.
Your room is doing very poor.
Sugar! There's your old puppet,
The one of Little Miss Muffet!
Your pencils are scattered in the closet.
There's the money you were supposed to deposit.
"But Mom, my room is clean!
How could you be so mean?
It's yours whose looks obscene!"
"Sugar, I was talking to your father.
It's him I have to bother!"

Emily Stegman
Age: 10

LIFE

Life is like a tornado
Spinning and spinning
Until it gets too weak
To blow anymore.

Life can be like a park bench
People will use sometimes
But all in all
You're mostly in society's way.

Life is like a mirror.
You can sometimes see yourself
And sometimes it's just there
To make a room smaller or bigger

Life is like a river
Floating up and down on an adventurous dream
'Til you arrive at the location where you began.

Life is like a light bulb.
You shine your heart, soul, mind, and body
And maybe, just maybe,
You touch someone's life.

Life is like a roller coaster
At one moment
You're going just as slow as you please
Then all of a sudden
You're sprawling towards death and everlasting drama.
Then you realize you made it through.

But just like a roller coaster
It must come to an end
Or maybe a new beginning.

Gregory Pittard
Age: 14

FRIENDS! FRIENDS! FRIENDS!

Friends are fun,
Friends are kind,
Friends are people who help you
When you're feeling blue.
Friends care about you,
Friends are cool, not bad,
You help a friend
When they are sad.

David Drees
Age: 9

RAIN

Rain, rain, I dislike the rain.
It rains so hard I nearly cry.
I will dislike the rain,
Until I gain power over the rain.

Ashley Nicole Anderson
Age: 9

ODE TO A JERSEY

I only wish I could give you more
than a clean wash and a hanging on the door.
You were more special than that.
Without you, the coach wouldn't let me bat.
Your numbers read so crisp and clear.
When they saw number two, the crowd gave a cheer.
You were there for the pop-ups, the throws, and the runs.
You were there on the bench with the hot dogs
and the buns.
I put you away with sorrow and grief.
My awesome sprained ankle made our season too brief.

Alex Moen
Age: 14

SPACE

Outer space, outer space
What a wonderful place

Jupiter is made out of gas
Saturn is not made of glass

Pluto is way out in space
The sun is a very hot place

Matthew Hott
Age: 9

KEEP ON TRUCKIN'

Don't let other people
Tell you what to do.
Don't fall into their standards
If that's not really you.

Be a freak or get straight A's
Do what it is you feel.
You won't amount to anything
If you can't take yourself for real.

Don't sell out for money
Don't sell out for grades.
Your morals will stay intact
While these things fade away.

Patricia Feghali
Age: 13

FOOD OH, FOOD

Food oh, food I love you, you're great.
Everything else are things I hate.
Food oh, food you're best of all.
You're better than a bat and ball.
Food oh, food I love you so.
Every time I think about you,
my heart starts to flow.

H. Ricky Allaer
Age: 8

TRUE LOVE

Bob was looking for a love,
A love that was as beautiful as a dove,
Like an angel that has come from above,
All that Bob wants is his true lady love.

Jane is very dazed and confused,
She has the love lost blues.
She has had many men in her life,
All of her men had no night life.

Bob and Jane were perfect matches,
Like a fisherman with two great catches.
They would be the perfect couple,
Together they were as sweet as a truffle.

When they got together,
Their love was as beautiful as a feather.
They finally got married,
Jane had to be carried, over the threshold.

Jamal Shteiwi
Age: 14

A FRIEND IS A FRIEND!!

A friend is a friend like friends should be.
A friend is a friend like you and me.

A friend likes to laugh or joke around.
A friend likes to talk or just go for a walk.

A friend will be there if you're happy or sad.
A friend will be there if you're angry or mad.

A friend will be there when you're down.
They'll jump up and down and act like a clown.

A friend will be there when you're all alone.
They'll call you up to talk on the phone.

When you're sick and home from school,
your friend will tell you that's okay
and they start to act cool.

A friend is someone special
who will help you write a book.
Then for paying them back
you can teach them how to cook.

I have a lot of friends, they are really nice,
we hope our friendship never ends.

A friend is a friend like friends should be,
a friend is a friend like you and me!!

Elizabeth Waltz
Age: 11

I stare deep into the fiery red-orange flames
Reality no longer exists
I'm enclosed inside the flames and everything is a blur
Those flames are all I can see
Spinning like a roller coaster inside my head
Suddenly, I snap back
I'm at the same peaceful setting I was at before
The warmth from the blazing inferno comforts me
Fresh kindling is fed to the fire
and it crackles with delight
It spits out sparks that scurry around aimlessly
before they slowly diminish
The cries of the night creatures echo
throughout the woods
I tilt my head back and gape in amazement at the heavens
"Man they are beautiful," I muse quietly
The cool night wind whistles throughout the site
She envelops me and I shiver
A sharp tingle is shot down my spine
A few of my closest peers are with me
to witness the beauty
We chew the fat awhile reminiscing about the past
The rackety old boom box still plays our favorite songs
"Pushing horns weren't easy,"
we begin reverently singing
"The Cowboy Song" in unison
We'll retire from our sojourn at dusk, and
As sure as the sun will rise tomorrow
We'll feel lousy from lack of sleep and low hygiene
But right now, life just doesn't get any better than this

David Robert Crookham
Age: 15

TROPICAL FISH

My tropical fish swim in the sea.
But they don't know reality.
So now they're in a very big tank
On a very high shelf
Away from a cat named Hank

Poor angelfish wouldn't stop flying
I couldn't be lying
I hope I never lose my fish
In the sea of reality

Ploy Keener
Age: 8

A POEM ABOUT THE FARM

A tractor is a tractor.
A barn is a barn.
Corn is corn.
Where is the horn?

Oh where could it be?
Could it be on a cow?
I don't know.
Could it be on a bull?
Well, at last it could be on a cow.

Laneisha Matthews
Age: 9

THE FLEA

A ppreciate what your friend does,
    don't ignore his achievements.

F riendly to other people,
    not just people he thinks are cool.
R eally interesting,
    not someone boring that doesn't ever do anything cool.
I n my point of view,
    doesn't think he's above everyone else
    mentally and physically.
E xcels in sports and plays at least two a year.
N ot a believer in stereotypes,
    doesn't think everyone should be like him.
    Thinks everyone should be different.
D oesn't think they're flawless, knows it's OK to make
    mistakes.

T wo of a kind, has a lot in common with me.
O n weekends is allowed to come over or go somewhere
    like a baseball game.

F unny, makes jokes that make sense and
    are really entertaining.
L ives on the edge, isn't afraid of everything,
    willing to do risky activities.
E xpects to get what he deserves,
    doesn't think he'll get away with everything.
A fraid of some things, not a fearless show-off.

Dedicated to: All my friends.

Curtis J. Eilers
Age: 11

MY NEIGHBORS

I have some good neighbors who live on a hill.
They have a big dog that never sits still.
He bit my kid sister and tore up our house,
And last time I saw him, he ate my new blouse.
I like my good neighbors, our friendship is sound,
But that dog of theirs, should go to the pound.

Emily Cortright
Age: 10

PEOPLE

People - big, small, short, and tall.
Enormous eyes of colors and size.
Skins of many colors, each slightly
Different in their own little world.
Homes of wood, brick, stone, or
Straw it really doesn't matter at all.
Some people - powerful and strong
But others not known at all.
Billions of human beings...
Young and old, sick and well,
Happy and unhappy, kind and unkind,
Strong and weak, known and unknown,
All in one unique world.

Rachel Tepe
Age: 12

HALLOWEEN

Halloween, Halloween, galore
There's a jack-o'-lantern beside my door
See the kids line up just right
There are too many

Off goes my light!

Maureen Hayes
Age: 11

THE GHOUL CREW

Ghosts and goblins and witches, too,
  are all part of a scary crew.
They come out on Halloween night
  to fill the streets with sounds of fright.
While witches cackle with delight
  and the moon casts shadows with an eerie light,
A pumpkin carved with a devilish grin
  sits back and waits for the fun to begin.
The ghosts all hover in the air
  and seem to whisper, "Children, beware!"
Skeletons sway in the gentle breeze;
  their rickety bones shake like dead tree leaves.
So before you go out trick-or-treating,
  be prepared for the ghouls you'll be meeting.

Stephen A Meyer
Age: 12

RAIN

When rain falls to the ground
Flowers weep all around,
And when I sit to pray
I hope it rains every day
Animals sit together in threes
Under the beautiful maple trees,
The dark, cloudy, gray skies
Always seem to be in disguise,
Everything is dreadfully wet
So I lie down and forget
That the clear skies are very near,
I hope the sun will hide in fear
Behind the clouds so faraway
I wish it would forever stay,
Even though the rain has to go
I hang my head very low,
I know it will come back soon,
As I watch the bright moon
I close my eyes and fall asleep
As I try not to weep.

Katie Klekamp
Age: 13

HALLOWEEN

I just love Halloween don't you?
There are ghosts, goblins, and witches too.
There are so many different costumes to see,
and at each house a different treat.
You can get dressed up in different outfits.
Will you get toys I surely doubt it.
But you will see ghosts, goblins and witches too.
I just love Halloween don't you?
Boo!

Kelly Kalb
Age: 8

AUTUMN

Autumn is a time of leaves,
Gently falling from fine oak trees.

Autumn is a time of color,
Peace and love sent to each other.

Autumn is a time of play,
Little kids who shout, "Hooray!"

Autumn is a time of art.
Sending a message to our heart.

Katherine Riestenberg
Age: 10

ONE OF THOSE DAYS

My alarm wakes me up at six in the morning,
I quickly turn it off and then I keep snoring.
But before I know, it's almost time to go,
So I'm rushing around as fast as I can go.

I just make the bus, after all of that rush.
But my seat has three: two others and me,
I'm in the middle and now I'm crushed.

I'm feeling a little better when I get to third bell.
I finally might be out of my bad spell.
But when I'm asked for my homework I feel so dumb,
Because it's now that I realize it's not all done.

It takes me three minutes to get to my locker
before sixth bell begins.
So I'm running down the stairs, and I'm almost there,
when suddenly the bell rings.

Finally, at last, it's the end of the day!
School is out (Hurray! Hurray!)!
But when I grab all of my stuff, and out I try to run,
I have to go slow because my backpack weighs a ton!

When I finally get to bed at night, I hope and I pray,
That tomorrow won't be another one of those days.

Alison Janine Bedingfield
Age: 12

THE PERFECT MAN

About two thousand years ago,
A man walked the earth.
A man who taught people to get along,
A man who taught people to work together,
A man who was created by the heavenly Father
to die for my sins.

A man who could heal the sick,
A man who could do miracles,
A man who sacrificed his life only because he wanted
to be my Savior.

A man who could walk on water,
A man who could calm the sea,
A man who was arrested just because he loved me.

A man who rose from the tomb,
A man who ascended into Heaven,
A man who was crucified only because he was perfect.

A man who was born of a virgin,
A man who was created to die,
A man who was the Son of God,
A man named Jesus.

He was the only perfect man,
To ever walk the earth,
So if I follow in his footsteps,
I will be perfect in the eyes of my Creator.

Kathleen Wilson Hart
Age: 12

HELP

Sometimes I feel so happy.
Sometimes I feel so sad.
Sometimes I feel so happy,
but lately I just feel bad.

I'm hurting inside and out.
All I seem to do is shout.
All I seem to do is pout.

Sometimes I get so mad,
'cause my life is such a drag.

Why can't someone help me,
through these troubled times.

Oh why can he not see,
there's someone hurting
and that someone is me.

Shiloh J. Roberts
Age: 14

FALL...

Fall is chilly weather,
Fall is leaves,
Fall is sweaters,
Fall is trees.

Fall is homework,
Fall is fun,
Fall is dark,
When the day is done.

Maria Ewing
Age: 11

I'M THANKFUL FOR FALL!

I'm thankful for fall,
Because people get a ring in their heads,
And jump into bed,
For tomorrow is Halloween.
When Halloween is over and
Thanksgiving is near,
Get ready to start another year.
When Thanksgiving is over,
And so is fall . . .
Get ready for next year,
And a brand new FALL!

Sarah E. McAdams
Age: 9

MY AUTUMN EYES BEHOLD

Vivid orange pumpkins that light up the night,
Leaves of all colors; mahogany, goldenrod, bittersweet,
Periwinkle sky that beholds flapping wings,
Dark brown squirrels burying their nuts,
Big trees holding just a few mysterious leaves.

Jessica McQuillan
Age: 9

SNOW

Falling crystals
falling,
falling,
From the heavens
From above,
Falling crystals
from the sky
falling,
falling,
Onto the ground.
That's where they rest
Forevermore,
That's where they rest
Forevermore.

Steven M. Gaulding
Age: 13

HUNGRY FOR THE SEAT

An average seventh grader
gathered with his friends
around the lunch table,
possessing the courage of a warrior
ready to battle to gain acceptance.

Wrapped in a thousand fears,
he prepares for the competition.
He is armed with gentle words
and a friendly disposition.

He knows words can strike like swords.
He received many wounds
enduring the pain that sometimes never ends.

The battle is won or lost
depending upon the seat.
Glory to the lucky one
who claims near the leader.
The closest is preferred.
Second prize if it is reserved.
Fatally wounded if excluded.
Today he conquered.
Tomorrow he must be ready again.

Nathan J. Powers
Age: 12

AUTUMN WINDS

As I walk down the dreary path,
the autumn wind blows softly through my hair,
And in the distance,
I hear chimes ringing through the air.
The wind through the trees
makes a soft howling sound,
Blowing leaves softly to the ground.
They swirl around my tired feet,
As if it were me they were supposed to greet.
As I approach my empty house,
I see no lights at all,
Just my gray horse to greet me,
neighing from its lonely stall.

How many autumns have I been alone?
How many dresses have I sewn?
Sitting by a dying fire on a cold and lonely night,
Trying not to seem lonely with all my heart and might.
But I am still alone with no one to talk to and
no one to listen to the stories I might have told.
I will always be alone every single day
even when I am weak and old.

But the autumn winds blow the years past,
And one year looks just like the last.
It would not be so bad, of course,
If someone else was here besides my horse.
Would anyone want me as their host?
Especially if I told them the truth, that I am a ghost.

Carrie Hathaway
Age: 12

BRUSSELS SPROUT PIE

Brussels sprout pie, I adore you.
You come in handy when there's nothing to do.
I'll bake a pie, a Brussels sprout pie.
My sweetheart will say, you're the true love of my eye.
Brussels sprout pie, I adore you.
You're a good thing to eat,
My heart belongs to you.

Courtney Grace
Age: 8

BASEBALL IS FUN

After the cold of winter is gone
And the warmth of spring makes green the lawn
Young boys and girls get out their gloves
To play the game they dearly love.

The older guys who get paid to play
Have all but ruined the game today
But we play for fun, and it upsets me to say
They're getting richer, we have to pay to play.

We like to field, but we love to bat
We look good in our uniforms, (yes, even the hats)
We throw, we catch, we hit, and we run
I can't wait 'til spring, baseball is fun.

Tony Focke
Age: 8

MY MOM IS MAD AT ME

My mom is mad at me you see
Because I broke the new TV
Because I wrecked my brother's teepee
Because I broke my sister's Barbie
My mom is mad at me.

Johnathon Vasiliadis
Age: 8

LOVE CONQUERS ALL

The tree sways to-and-fro,
As a lovely maiden there sat.
She sat so weeping
Over her lost love.
Her love went off to war
And there was slain.
They carried his body to her
And she saw his cold unloving face.
And now that he is gone
She will follow her heart.
Within a moment she too will be
A lost soul in the underworld.
But she will be with her love
And he with her.
Together their souls intertwined forever.

Elizabeth Carullo
Age: 14

MERRY-GO-ROUND

I'm riding on a merry-go-round,
My feet won't ever touch the ground,
Because I'm riding a merry-go-round.

Amy Jo Kellems
Age: 8

HALLOWEEN

H ave you seen ghosts and goblins?
A ll of you must run.
L ast night my friend ran.
L ater he ran again but no
O ne saw him.
W hen Halloween arrived
E veryone was ready.
E veryone except
N athan., finally
  He was ready.
  Then he met a ghost.
  He was frightened.
  He was so frightened that he ran away.
  That's why I said to run.

Michael Federle

GRANDPA

I love you Poppy.
Poppy you are the best
Grandpa in the world.
Remember when we went to the zoo?
That was fun.
I remember in the morning when you came,
I kept asking you for some of your coffee cake.
That was cool.
I remember when you died.
I just sat there and cried.
Jamey held me and said Miki,
I know he is dead but he will always love you
and I thought I heard you say I love you
and I started crying all over again.

Miki Flynn
Age: 9

OH, NO! I'M LATE!

Oh, no! I'm late,
I'm late for school,
I feel like a fool.
My mom was supposed to drive me
but she can't find the keys.
If I'm late for school
I'll get a week's D.T.'s.
Hurry up, hurry up!
Pick up your feet!
If I'm late for school
I'll be dead meat!

Cameron Sakurai

HALLOWEEN

Halloween is very scary with ghosts,
and goblins and monsters that are hairy.

Late at night when you are asleep,
that is when the monsters begin to creep.

But, the reason I think Halloween is dandy
is because you gets lots and lots of candy.

Shawn Thomas

A CAT AS ITS OWN PERSON

It's amazing,
How the cat curls and slides,
Through lazy people's feet they wind,
Gracefully leaping from chair to table to floor.

They quietly clean themselves in a corner,
Washing away their troubles,
Sinister eyes glance around,
Looking for comfort,
In some child's lap.

Erin Jennifer Morgan
Age: 10

FREEDOM

What is freedom?
Is freedom soaring high like the eagle,
running wild like the wolf,
swinging swiftly like the chimp,
crawling slowly like the slug,
hopping happily like the hare,
or is freedom what you and I do every day?
What is freedom?
Is there such a thing?

Kelly Klocke
Age: 12

WATERLOO

Riding along, oblivious to the screams and yells.
Riding along, the scent of cannon he could smell.
Riding along, through an explosion and a spray of dirt.
Riding along, not feeling anything, not getting hurt.
Through the men, upon his steed.
Through the death while gathering speed.
Through the blue and then beyond.
Through the French, while wanting a calm.
Slash! Stab! Yet another one down.
Slash! Stab! On his face grows a frown.
Slash! Stab! Yet another one down.
Can he bear it? No, he can't. Shall he continue?
No, he shan't.
Stopping, for God's call.
Stopping, letting himself fall.
Stopping, not to defend.
Stopping, here comes the end.
The end, soldiers running all around.
The end, feet thundering towards him on the ground.
The end, he can sense the oncoming pain.
The end, his withdrawal from war has been in vain.

John Henry Newman
Age: 12

THE SILENCE CLUB

Silence fills the mourning yard,
The members take their seats.
A new member has come to join the club,
The living cry and weep.
The members silently sit and wait,
For the ancient ritual is about to begin.
As soon as the living leave the yard,
The members come out of the ground.
Their job is an important one,
Their message is silently transferred,
From each mute mouth, to each deaf ear.
The new member feels important words,
That he heeds with all respect.
The words that he hears go like this:
"You have joined our Silence Club,
The fraternity of the ages.
Once a member always a member,
We really have but one rule.
Which you will obey and you must obey,
Your sentence has begun.
And here is our rule which you must obey:
No sounds in the Silence Club."

Kate Gehring
Age: 13

SHE

With her bright crown of gold and
Her magic wand of wander,
She tells the world to change
Without one hint of a blunder.

On her throne of glory, she tells us her story,
Of how the wind blows and why the grass grows.

She begins with the spring, where all is green,
And the flowers have just started to bloom,
The rabbits are hopping, the sky is not sopping,
With one ounce of wet, grimy gloom.

When the weather grows warmer,
And the leaves are fully grown,
The small creek acts as a performer,
And gives us a show of its own.

But with one turn of her key,
The leaves turn from green to red,
And as far as the eye can see,
The world is the beauty that she said.

And when the autumn breezes blow
From chillier to very cold,
The branches on the leaves begin to break
And die and tear and fold.

But then one misty morning, she sends from the stars,
A white powdered flow that we call snow.

And when the whole world is tucked away in her sheet,
Mother Nature thinks of the next season to meet.

Laura Carver
Age: 13

There was a guy who owned a store
Who made pies and pies galore
He met his customers at the door
Then he told of his flowers and a lot more
He told them of his hopes and dreams and fears
At times he even shed a few tears
When a withering woman came in
with doubt on her face
He took her around and showed
her his place
He gave her some pie and put a
smile on her face
He took her to dinner at a wondrous place
Then that night they both got maced
They went to the hospital and
then sang Amazing Grace
From then on they worked on
that famous corner
And laughed and laughed
about Little Jack Horner

Steven Tabar
Age: 12

ZLATA'S DIARY, A POEM ABOUT THE BOOK

This story is about,
a little girl with doubt.
Her family was fine,
until love and hate combine.
Her town was invaded,
and things seemed X-rated.
They all seemed forgotten,
and their lives became rotten.
Zlata never thought things would turn out this way,
and it all ruined her birthday.
Sarajevo will never forget,
this time of regret,
When love and hate combined.
Everyone is sad,
since things were so bad.
Troops were sent,
and a long time they spent.
People cried,
as children died.
They waited for days and I think that is rude,
all of that time waiting for one box of food.
The streets were not safe for children to play,
day, by day, by day....
Still things are messy,
and people are testy.
People will not laugh, and people will not cry,
for now their lives are ever so dry.
Sarajevo will never be the same,
for that life of theirs once was so tame.
Zlata's town was like a happy clown,
and now, everyone's spirits are down.
They all needed a friend, and we helped to lend

a reaching hand to them.
People say,
that they are still in dismay.
And because they were hated,
their lives have totally faded.
And if you care enough,
then we can help buff....up their lives today!!!

Katie Keers
Age: 13

GO THE DISTANCE

Let us walk to support America,
Let us walk to be free,
Let us walk for each other,
In peace and harmony.

We shall help out when we are called to it,
We shall help out anyone,
If we all do a little bit,
The job will get done.

Now all shall go the distance,
Every single one,
Now everyone made a difference,
Finally, peace has begun.

Whitney Botsford

SWEET FIFTEEN

A world is seen
through tear stained eyes.
The mighty gods
have fallen.
Ideas come into a place
once naive,
and lullabies have lost their lull.

Friends offer safe havens peace,
which the immediates
don't seem to provide.
Love is not as understanding
as it is in the books,
and Suzy Snowflake dies.

Life is not the fairy tale
that somehow we all believe.
Childish games
have lost their luster
as well as those fantastical dreams.

Mighty mountains
become small hills
and the jungle gym
too small.
Santa Claus has ceased to come
and the Easter Bunny no longer calls.

Cindy Merle
Age: 16

TIME

What is this thing that we call time?
That's the topic of this rhyme.

Where did it come from, and how did it get here?
These complex issues only add to our fear.

It's been here forever, I tell you no lie.
It has no beginning and it won't ever die.

It tells us what to do from day to day.
It tells us when to eat, sleep, work, and play.

We make no plans without time's permission.
A week long vacation or a day out fishin'.

It controls every aspect of our daily life.
It puts pressure on us and adds to our strife.

Seconds, minutes, hours, days.
These units of time put our plans in a haze.

So much to do, how will it get done?
These busy schedules take from us our fun.

So, what's the moral of this little rhyme?
Just keep taking life one day at a time.

Matthew Larson
Age: 16

I SAW SOMETHING IN THE SKY!

I saw something in the sky
   I tried to say "Hi."
      But it just went on not listening to me.
I wish, oh, how I wish,
    I could fly like a bat
And fly like cats without a broom.
     They wouldn't care
      They just fly everywhere
     I spy, and I say "Bye"
But all the witches just say "Hi!"

Natalie A. McGary
Age: 5

AUTUMN

Flowers and leaves are fading now.
Wilting plants to the ground floor below,
Weather's changing from rain to snow,
OH! How the autumn winds blow!

Our rakes are working hard and long,
Many birds sing an autumn song,
Cornstalks are standing high and tall,
How the children like the fall.

Brandon Nutting
Age: 12

A WITCH

A witch is flying high in the sky.
She is so scary,
That you could cry.

She and her cat are on a broom,
You can see her from the window in your room.

You dread the night she'll come and haunt your house,
And turn you into a tiny mouse.

Then she'll eat you and you'll be gone,
And she'll keep your parents as her pet fawn.

Katharine Ciliberti
Age: 8

SEASONS

Summer, winter, spring, and fall
Makes you think of birthdays and all.
I think Christmas is the best.
Season's greetings from the guests.
Fall is nice, so is spring.
I think summer is the strangest thing.
I like fall because of all the leaves.
People have tricks up their sleeves.

Jessica York
Age: 8

THE WITCHES

They are always in the sky.
Flying really high.
Over the house. In the car.
By my dog named Candy Bar.

Aaron Lee Slusher
Age: 9

WHAT DO I DO?

Do I do this?
Do I do that?
Should I copy?
Should I not?
What do you do on this question?
Do I write?
Do I draw?
Do I guess but should I not?
Do I quit?
Do I not?
Is it hard?
Yes it is really hard.
Can't you tell?
Not even the smartest smarty
Can figure this out!
Guess what grade I got!

Kevin Rauch
Age: 9

Train, train down the Chicago Line,
working, working against time.
Huffing and puffing and working hard,
trying to stay by the schedule card.

People are going to be late,
if the train doesn't accelerate.
What will the people do?
The only people that know are me and you.

The train pulls up at half past eight,
"Wow, this train is really late!"
The conductor yells really hard,
"Please may I see your passport card."

One person doesn't have it,
he'll be sent back to Habit.
All the others had theirs,
they don't have any cares.

When the train leaves again,
it will go to the city Len.

Train, train down the Chicago Line,
working, working against time.
Chugging and puffing and working hard,
trying to stay by the schedule card.

Christa Wessels
Age: 10

83

ANGRY

I was angry when she knocked me down.
I know she tripped me then,
When I cut my chin.

She was there laughing away,
While I had a sore chin the rest of the day.

She was also the one who pushed me in the mud,
That old Mary Jane Anne McCudd.

She is always there when I trip or stumble.
That's why I know she's behind all this trouble.

Krysten Williams
Age: 9

AUTUMN

Autumn is a time that leaves fall on the ground
Autumn is a time to kick the soccer ball around
Autumn is a time to go trick-or-treating
Autumn is a time that families have Thanksgiving eating
Autumn is a time to rake colorful leaves
Autumn is a time to wear long sleeves
When autumn is over, I feel very, very sad
Because when winter comes, I am not at all glad.

Bridget Dean
Age: 10

BIRDS

Birds, birds,
they fly in the sky.
They have an aerial view of an orange, an apple,
and even a pizza pie.
Feathers on their wings make them fly well,
for without them, a long time ago they would have fell.
Their houses are made of sticks and twigs;
they fly to the south to escape the cold winds.
Birds, birds,
they are the best,
they fly in the air on a magical quest!

Sheraz S. Anwar
Age: 12

OUR HIKE

Early this summer me and my family
went down South to see the clear sky.
We wanted to hike to the Natural Bridge.
My dad said he knows the way along the ridge.
Over the hill and across the creek.
Before I knew it my shoes had a leak.
We walked for an hour with my feet all wet.
We had to get back before the sun set.

Randi Barber
Age: 8

I USED TO BE A NON-CONFORMIST

I used to be a non-conformist,
my imagination ran wild.
I used to be a non-conformist,
I never followed another child.

Then one day that all changed.
People looked at me and said,
"Boy, isn't that kid strange?"
Unfortunately I let them get to my head.

I used to be a non-conformist,
I always dressed a different way.
I used to be a non-conformist,
until that awful day.

I wanted to be different from the others,
but I didn't want to be called "strange."
So I ended up like all of the others,
not having my own opinion.

Now I am a conformist,
I should have never let them get to my head.
Because without my opinion,
I'm as good as dead.

Brandon Sheckels
Age: 12

WILD THING

Patches is a good old dog.
She loves to play and chew.
But every time we turn around.
She's got somebody's shoe.

Lindsay Gaertner
Age: 8

TRICK-OR-TREAT

I go trick-or-treating
Every Halloweeny.
When I go "rat-rat"
I scare a cat and a bat.

Jennifer Rahlmann
Age: 8

UNIQUE FINGERS, BORING TOES

Ten fingers and ten toes I have
Ten fingers and ten toes.
But if you really think about
Those ten fingers and ten toes;
You finally figure out - wait,
Of fingers there's only eight.
You see I forgot the most important
Those door opening thumbs.
Now feet don't have any thumbs.
Nope, they got toes.
And of your eight remaining fingers
Only six should count.
I mean your pinky, what's up with that.
It sits there by itself, while it looks for a love pat,
It hides the gifts of the others.
The index, the middle, and the ring.
The latter stands for commitment,
While the index is just for pointing out.
That final one is shown
By people driving on the expressway.
There are ten toes but only six unique fingers,
Each with its own name.
They feel every little thing
For they are our second eyes.
And when in doubt I close my eyes.
Not a second thought do I give,
I place a pen inside those fingers;
I give them space to move,
And I let my fingers do the walking.

Tareq Abdulghani
Age: 13

A LOVELY LASS

A lovely lass lived in South Carolina,
Susan Smith, mother of two.
Once happily married and content,
Now is the time her actions are to rue.

She had a husband who left her,
A new love who wanted to leave.
Night after night she tossed and turned,
Mentally ill and destined to grieve.

I don't want children he once said.
She wanted to please him so he would stay,
She devised a plan to please him,
So they could be together forever and a day.

She accused a man of kidnapping her children,
On TV she made her plea.
The nation sorrowed with this mother,
When she confessed it was agony.

Lauren E. Grote
Age: 13

LUNATIC!!

There once was a loon
Who stared at the moon.

He would pull gourds.
And drive a Ford.

He was born in June
Just like Bret Boone.

He would read cookbooks
When fish were on his hooks.

He would go out west
When he looked his best.

He liked to chew gum
He thought it was fun?

Lunatic! Lunatic! Lunatic!

Nathan Herrington
Age: 10

ONE HUNDRED FEET TALL

If you were one hundred feet tall
You would not be very small.
When you drool,
You would make a pool.
Kids would think you were very cool!
If you were one hundred feet tall.

When you go out to play,
Kids would run away.
You would squash a mouse,
If you lived in his house.
This poem was hard to write because
I'm one hundred feet tall.

Kevin A. Heasley
Age: 10

BUSY BEE

Busy bees are working on honey.
They just love making honey.
They love making honey because it gives them money.
You need money to buy honey.
It can't be too runny.
They work best when it's sunny.
Sometimes bees are funny.

Curtis Bosch
Age: 8

CHRISTMAS CHEER

What a fun day Christmas is!
It'll be the best day of this year!
We'll be playing,
We'll be laughing,
And we'll even be praying.
Time to sing, and dance,
It's celebrated even in France!
We always thought it was pretty fun,
In winter,
There is no sun.
St. Nick will soon be here,
We'll be filled with
Christmas cheer!

Nina Baker
Age: 8

RAINY DAY

It's a rainy day and there's nothing to do.
It's a rainy day and it's so blue too.
The birds are not singing and the sun is not shining.
Oh what will I do on this rainy rainy day.

Frannie Nolan
Age: 9

RAIN

It is fun and wet.
Children like to play in it.
Rain makes plants grow now.

Ashley N. Haun

CAPTAIN SNOW

Here lies the bones of Captain Snow.
He turned white and red then said "Ho, Ho."
On a special night it was zero below.
He saw a fire and started to blow.
That was the end of Captain Snow.

Stephanie Lynn Howe
Age: 10

Linda
Long hair
Likes playing soccer
She is really tall
Lin

Amanda Lynn Kyle
Age: 8

EARTH

Earth has birds and trees and bees,
But most of all earth is for me.
Reptiles, bats and ground and sky,
Earth just makes me want to fly.
People are just like me,
In America we are free!
Earth is fun, earth is cool
And God does rule.

Tyler Damon
Age: 8

This fall day is warm enough,
It's a good thing I'm round and tough.
The girls are screaming their team cheer,
The game begins as they come near.
The whistle blows, I'm in the air,
Where I go north or south.
Around the field, back and forth,
The net comes closer,
Before my eyes.
I'm then kicked harder,
Until I fly.
The goal is scared,
The game is over.
My life in soccer,
Goes on forever.

Suzie Koepfer
Age: 10

THAT SMELLY GAK

That smelly gak, it smells really bad
That smelly gak is making me mad
That smelly gak, I hate it a lot
That smelly gak is really hot
That smelly gak is really dumb
That smelly gak, it looks like gum
That smelly gak is really old
That smelly gak is not even sold!

Brian Englert
Age: 8

NATURE

Creatures
Foliage
Blossoms
Soaring birds
Climbing ivy
Strong, beautiful, magnificent trees
Those are just a few
Gliding leaves
Racing rabbits
Quick, slick, amazing fish
Stout toadstools too
Last of all, best of all,
I like majestic nature

Tim Severyn
Age: 11

The winter snow melts
So flowers can bloom
Birds build their nests
So their babies have room
The sun becomes warmer
Tree buds burst out
Spring finally arrives
Let's all give a shout

Julie Koepfer
Age: 10

There once was a man named Joe
He had a very large toe.
His dog's name was Moe.
Moe stepped on the toe of Joe.
And that's how Joe got a very large toe.

Lacy J. Pez
Age: 11

BASKETBALL

I like basketball
even though I'm not tall
I am a guard
I play in my yard
Basketball is fun
I play in the sun
Pass, pass, pass the ball
Dribble, dribble, dribble the ball
Dribble down the court
Basketball is a fun sport
You should try it
You will learn bit by bit
It is really fun
And maybe when you are done....
YOU WILL HAVE MANY TROPHIES,
More than one!

Gina Candelaresi
Age: 12

THE EARTH

The earth was once spinning in space,
A nice smooth ball,
Long before it became,
A home to us all.

Then millions more years,
Until the first plants and trees,
And small living things,
Crawled away from the seas.

Last came the people,
Young and old,
All different colors,
Bright and bold.

We need to take care,
Of this home we share,
And protect big and small,
This home to us all.

Erin Pleuss
Age: 11

THE WINTER WITCH

The Winter Witch is so mean
she goes around without being seen.

The little children cry and say no more.
But the witch says without snow
the world would be a bore.

She doesn't have a care
she just looks at the kids and plays with her hair.

The witch's heart is so black
when she misses a spot she goes right back.

This witch sings and dances
while the children take their glances.

So the witch will stay mean
with her black cat who is tending.
But still there is no happy ending.......

Tony Rue
Age: 11

WHEN I WAS A LITTLE GIRL...

When I was a little girl,
My grandmother told my mother,
Many things were different,
For people respected each other.

They lived much simpler lives back then,
And hardly ever had to hurry,
The kids could play outside at night,
Without causing the parents to worry.

Everyone in the family helped with the chores,
And the neighbors helped out too,
I wish life now was more like that,
Instead of all shiny and new.

When I was a little girl,
My mother has said to me,
Boys could go out and get dirty,
But girls, young ladies, must be.

We didn't have microwaves or computers,
No Nintendos, CDs, or tapes,
Milk was delivered to our back door,
And no one had heard of seedless grapes.

When I was a little girl,
I'll tell my daughter some day,
The earth was not so crowded;
Kids had yards in which to play.

We had mail delivered by hand to our house,
And a newspaper every afternoon,

Everything wasn't done by computers,
And man got no further in space than the moon.

There was no cure for cancer or AIDS,
From these many died.
We used fossil fuels to run machines,
Stop this pollution, many cried.

We all have our own stories to tell,
About the things that we've been through,
Tell yours and ask about someone else's
They'll be glad to talk with you.

Cynthia Carol Berning
Age: 12

BASKETBALLS BOUNCING

Balls are bouncing,
Girls are zooming,
Everyone is having fun!
Feet are pounding,
Whistles are blowing,
Hurry, hurry, run!
We're down by a point,
The clock's still ticking,
The ball goes in, we won!

Michelle Gundlach
Age: 9

A WRITER

I fall asleep,
And in my dream I see a person,
Vaguely familiar;
Myself in twenty years.
I am a writer,
Creator of stories, teller of tales.
Thoughts flow as freely as words on the paper,
Letting go.
Wandering in a world all my own,
Plot twisting and turning at my command.
I imagine the characters, but they tell the story,
I am only a watcher, an onlooker.

When my first manuscript is written,
I prepare it for the publisher,
Anxious for my career
To take wing.
I remember when I was a little girl
So long ago!
I wondered if I really wanted to be a writer.
I loved to write then, I still do.
It comes naturally, and I'm content.

Now my thoughts are interrupted
By a sound, startlingly real.
I turn off my alarm clock,
Getting up to go to school.
The dream, the vision is gone,
But never forgotten.

Elizabeth Ann Darbie
Age: 12

Painted red flowers
Bloom in the very warm spring
They are beautiful

Nick Oppenheim
Age: 10

FEELINGS

People laugh,
People cry,
All your feelings
Are inside.
Let them out,
And be about,
All the things
That make
You pout.

Lisa Ann Green
Age: 13

SANTA'S JOB

On New Year's Day, Santa Claus assigns each elf a
  child to watch to see
if he or she is good or bad.
Nobody knows this,
  because the elves are actually hiding under your bed.
  Why else does your mom say that you shouldn't keep
junk under there?
December first, all of the elves go back to the North Pole,
giving a list of the good and bad the child has done.
For two weeks, the elves work on making,
  wrapping, and
  putting cards on each gift.
They sing and dance,
drinking Mrs. Claus' delicious hot chocolate.
Santa helps a bit too.
On the night before Christmas, the elves attach all of the
  reindeer on the sleigh,
load all of the gifts,
and somehow make room for Santa.
So this Christmas Eve, go to bed early,
and don't forget to leave
  Santa some cookies and milk.

Saleha Ghani
Age: 12

FOOTBALL

Football is my favorite sport,
It is fun,
Playing all day,
Under the sun.

I play football,
All day long,
And when I play,
I sing a song.

I get hit hard,
By big boys,
I hit the ground so hard,
It feels like falling on a toy.

But that won't stop me because,
Playing football is my life,
If it was taken away from me,
It would be like stabbing me with a knife.

David Marquez
Age: 12

FOURTH OF JULY

Crash, drop, flash, pop,
crackle, bang.
Fourth of July is such an
exciting day.

Andrew Cunningham
Age: 11

A RAINBOW TELLS

A rainbow tells a story so sweet,
a story of pretty parakeets.

A rainbow is filled with beautiful colors,
it also has many wonders.

An ocean is clear, calm, and quiet,
as I sit solemnly beside it.

The river is so much like the ocean,
but the river has more motion.

Giant rapids wash me ashore
As I drift away I feel cold and sore.

The world has many beautiful things to deliver,
parakeets, rainbows, oceans, and rivers.

Brooke Holman
Age: 11

BRIGHT NATURE

Early morning I felt a breeze
Thought I heard the sea sneeze
Large birds in the sky
I wonder what it's like to fly
Every day I see heavenly green
Then I look at a pine lean

Hello bird in the sky
How high can you fly
What's it like in the blue
Where nothing touches you
Bird can you soar with your wings flat
While you're escaping a hungry cat

Daniel Curtis
Age: 12

BOOKS

A good thing when you want to quiet down,
Books make smiles out of frowns.
I think mysteries are the best,
But that doesn't stop me from reading the rest.
Books come alive when you read,
They give you happiness that you need.
Books give someone something to do,
I suggest a book for you!

Corey Anderson
Age: 12

LIKE A ROCKET

Like a rocket
I want to zoom
Here to there
Then there to here

I want to see
All there is to see
And more

I want to be
All I can be
And more

Like a rocket I want to be
Seeing things
That no one sees

I want to know things
That no one knows
I want to find something new

Like a rocket
I want to zoom
Here to there
Then there to here.

Christine Barrick

THAT GOOEY STUFF IN MY HOUSE

That gooey stuff is in my house.
It is very scary.
It scares my mom and dad.
That gooey stuff is hot.
That gooey stuff looks like gum.
That gooey stuff is on the furniture.
That gooey stuff is everywhere!!!!!

Alex Uphus
Age: 9

THE CHRISTMAS CALL

Christmas is the best time of the year,
A time for families to be near.
The snow outside is falling,
I think I hear the sleigh bells calling.

Lying by the firelight,
In hopes that we will see St. Nick tonight.
On the mantle our stockings lay,
Tomorrow will be the happiest day.

The next morning our eyes open wide,
We see many presents by our side.
The joy of the holiday brings warmth to all
As we answer the Christmas call.

Meagan Hawkins
Age: 14

AQUAMARINE

Aquamarine is the color of the sea,
The place where I would like to be.
The Statue of Liberty gives it a hint,
The color of aquamarine like a mint.
The color of the sky after a rain,
The color of a bruise after the pain.

Allison Hebeler
Age: 13

LOVE

A rose when illness calls,
Chocolates for no special reason,
A champagne meal at midnight,
Leaving letters outside one's halls.

The engagement ring, sparkling bright,
The wedding glowing with love,
After five years the love endures,
And fifty years prove delight.

Love can conquer war,
The humblest of all actions,
And one will know when it occurs,
When it reaches one's very core.

Maggie Collins
Age: 14

'TIS THE SEASON

Snow is falling,
children are laughing,
parents are busy trying
to finish their wrapping.
The stores are all closed,
everyone has gone home.
Families are together,
to celebrate forever,
the season of giving,
the season of living.
The birth of Christ is
upon this day,
the children will laugh,
and forever will they play.
What season is this?
It is the one you can't miss!
For Christmas is the season,
the season of giving,
the season of living.

Lauren Elizabeth Welsh
Age: 13

CHESTER

Chester is a cat that lives in the Monroe house.
He is such a scaredy-cat that he is afraid of a mouse.

Chester knows a dog Harold that is his best friend,
They talk about the Monroes over and over again.

All day long, Chester sleeps and sleeps,
So at night, he watches Bunnicula and
he gives Chester the creeps.

Chester knows about vampires because
he reads a lot,
So he thinks Bunnicula is a vampire
because he has weird spots.

Chester tries to warn the Monroes about
the vampire bunny,
By putting on a cape and biting Harold
in the neck, and everybody thinks that
he is funny.

Mario Francis Collini
Age: 10

I WANTED . . .

I wanted to play outside
but it's raining

I wanted to fall asleep
but I'm wide awake

I wanted to live in love
but I live in fear

I wanted to run away
but the streets can kill

I wanted to imagine
but I have no thoughts

I wanted to end my life
but I'm scared of death

I wanted to fly away
but my spirit died

I wanted to dream my dreams
but I get nightmares

Lindsay Masters
Age: 14

PONDEROUS THOUGHTS
ON A COLD, QUIET NIGHT

As the cool, crisp wind swept around her,
She stood there waiting.
For what, I did not know.
Could it be that jolly, fat red guy?
Or just a late December snow?

As she stood there alone that cold night
I suddenly heard a jingle off in the distance.
Soon, small, white, sparkling crystals
Started to fall from the sky.

As the jingles came closer
I felt a spark of excitement about the season
And the crystals came floating down faster.

I stood watching her and pondered
What Christmas was really all about.
Oh, how we sparkle it up!
Dazzling lights on houses,
Major sales at the stores,
Department store Santas.

But going deeper;
The gathering of loved ones,
Gifts for one another,
Feasting on roast beef and ham,
The birth of baby Jesus,
Special Christmas services at churches,
Wonderful songs shared and sung together.

I wondered if she was thinking the same thing.
Christmas is not just all bright lights and presents,
But a time for love, caring, giving, celebrating.

Diane Ulmer
Age: 12

THE VET

Alone in the graves so deep and wide,
Lie silent soldiers side-by-side.
Their spirits have gone from this world,
But in our hearts, memories of their death still whirl.

Their times may have quickly fled,
But we shall never forget how they bled.
We shall honor them forevermore,
And comfort their loved ones whose hearts are still sore.

Alyson Zureick
Age: 11

FRIENDSHIP

Friendship means playing and having fun.
Friendship means loving.
Friendship means caring.
Friendship means helping.
Friendship means always being there.
Friendship means laughing together.
Friendship means spending a whole day together.

Jena Hygema
Age: 9

SUN AND MOON

The sun and moon are like cat and dog
  Always playing tag.
They chase each other back and forth
  Behind mountains and clouds.
When one admits defeat
  The other dances with pride.
Those two never stop playing
  Even through the night.
The sun throws rays against the moon
  Which bounce in every way.
So when you see two animals playing
  Don't interrupt their game.
For they are like the sun and moon
  Playing their never-ending game.

Katie Woliver
Age: 11

Mrs. Keck and Mrs. Stockdell
are the best teachers in the world.
They are very nice and pretty and kind and neat.
Coolest in the universe and on Goyer Street.

Ashley Atkinson
Age: 8

SANTA CLAUS, SANTA CLAUS

Santa Claus, Santa Claus
December twenty-fifth,
presents in my stocking,
coming from the roof,
cookies on a plate,
milk in a glass,
for when Santa comes he'll get first class!
I in my night cap,
the tree all lit with lights on Christmas Eve,
It's a wonderful night.

Adrian Perrin
Age: 8

FREE THROW

The tall boy put his toes on the thin blue line.
The referee throws him the ball.
The crowd is silent as he looks at the rim.
He bounces the ball on the hardwood floor.
He shoots.
The ball bounces off the rim, and they lose the game.

John Popson
Age: 13

DOG HAIR EVERYWHERE

Dog hair everywhere,
On the floor,
Under the chair,
Behind the door,
Up the stairs,
In the corners,
In my hair,
Through the corridor,
On my sister's teddy bear.
Cleaning up is such a chore!
If you have a dog,
You better beware
Of dog hair everywhere!

Megan Lindley
Age: 14

THE SHADOW

I was sleeping one night,
When I saw a shadow,
All glowing with fright.
And to my surprise,
It was only my dad,
Who is very wise.
He came to my door and shut off my light,
And all of a sudden I became afraid of the night.
The shadow returned with all its might,
It was only my sister tiptoeing in the night.
I pulled the covers up over my head,
And then I saw the sun gazing over my bed.
Boy am I glad the night is over,
But I still want to go back under my cover.

Arin Shae Zehner
Age: 12

SOME FRIENDS

Some friends care,
some friends share,
but some only look at your outerwear.
Some friends say "yes" while others say "no,"
but the best friends of all are the ones you really know.

Brock McMillen
Age: 13

GOALIE

Rough, tough
Game saver
Point stopper
Free as a bird
in the wind
running fast
diving, blocking
Punting the ball
No shot passes
No one scores

Jamie Baumgart
Age: 11

VOLLEYBALL

This sport is very fun.
You can play it on the beach in the sun.

Bump, spike, set
over the net!

A high five goes to our team
and a "Good Job" to the other team.

And...remember you don't have to run
to have fun!!!

Tiffany F. Foster
Age: 12

CHEERLEADING

We encourage them to win, win, win,
Fans fill the stands
Waving our pom poms all around
We tumble, we jump,
We scream for the team!
That's what cheering's all about.

Misty Lea Hunter
Age: 11

THE RIVER IN THE TREES

As I scan my mind,
in a far back time,
I think of the trees,
the trees that I see,
with all other life,
serene, without strife,
I now remember the river.
The river in the trees,
with those tall, green trees,
without a fear that can make you quiver,
not a fear that can make you shiver,
all this by the river in the trees,
all this by the river in the trees.

Matthew Weaver
Age: 12

RAINBOWS

Rainbows have many colors,
Red stands for love,
the love that fills the world.
Orange stands for peace,
the peace that fills the universe.
Yellow stands for sunshine,
the brightness that is possible in everyone's day.
Green stands for life,
the life that God created.
Blue stands for eternity,
that is God's promise to his people.
Purple stands for unity,
that guides us to GOD'S KINGDOM.

Katya Kae Price
Age: 13

DON'T LOOK AT ME

Don't look at me, please don't stare.
Am I so rare that you must stare?
If you must look, see with your eyes the pain
In my heart. After you have done this, then
You may judge me for who I am inside.

Brooke Marie McMillen
Age: 13

MYSELF

My name is Brachla Messersmith.
I am a very smart girl.
I like to dance and play.
I love to read.
I have a dog.
I have a friend named Whitney.
I love the United States of America.
I want to be a doctor,
   So I can be a mother.

Brachla Messersmith
Age: 8

MICHAEL JORDAN IS THE BEST

Michael Jordan is the best
he shoots three pointers like none of the rest.
When he goes up, you can tell he is shooting.
By the time you're ready, he is moving right past.
Michael Jordan is the best.

Michael Jordan is very good at shortening leads,
gaining leads, and scoring.
Michael Jordan is the best.

But most of all, Michael Jordan is good at burning
people with his fake, double pump and reverse.
Air Jordan is the best.

Anthony Newman
Age: 12

THE SUSPECT OF A CRIME

A murderer who has made a kill
Did it with a thrill.
Finally a suspect is caught,
And his life begins to rot.
As he puts his hands on the bars
He thinks of escaping, but he knows he
Won't get far.
For now he lies in a prison cell
With a shocking secret he will not tell.
He knows he has done no wrong,
But nevertheless, he will be killed
At the crack of dawn.
Soon the real killer will strike again,
And nobody knows where or when.

John G. Maijub
Age: 12

THE COOL MULE

The mule went to school
To see a fool,
But he saw a tool,
Then saw a fool
And he said, "Cool!"

Whitney Renee Blair
Age: 7

BIRDS

Birds are big or very small
They pick at everything that crawls
They make a nest that looks dull.

Not all birds are like this,
not a sea gull not at all
A sea gull eats fish not things that crawl
It has a beak that looks almost ten feet tall

Birds can fly yes they can
They can fly to Brazil and,
back again
They fly all day
They fly all night
and never crash while in flight.

Timothy Mark Hartinger
Age: 12

POLLUTION

I really hate pollution,
    it is very bad.
I really hate pollution,
it makes me very mad.

I really hate pollution,
    it's bad to the earth.
I really hate pollution,
for nothing is it worth.

I really hate pollution,
    it gets into the air.
I really hate pollution,
    it isn't very rare.

Nick A. Fishback
Age: 12

RETURN OF THE MUMMY!

He's back from the dead
and he wants your head
You can run but you can't hide
because this mummy wants you fried
If you don't want to die
you better learn how to fly
If he finds you and has his way
that surely will make his day
Then he'll make the world pay
for what happened to him an earlier day
He got them and he'll get you
so you better watch what you do!

Greg S. Gallimore
Age: 11

MYSELF

I climbed up in a tree,
  up high!
I saw a bird flying by,
  a jet go by so high in the sky.
I climbed back down and went inside.

Whitney Carmichael
Age: 8

LIVE

Why are we here?
What is our purpose?
What can we do?
We can do anything.
We can live.

Laura C. Krizmanich
Age: 13

C ats are my favorite animals.
L oving person.
A pples are my favorite fruit.
I like the color green.
R achael is my middle name.
E ggs are my favorite food.

Claire Scheidler
Age: 8

I love the summer.
The woodpecker sounds like a drummer.
Today is very hot,
But today my problems I have forgot.
Today everyone is at the beach.
Off in a distance, I can hear the hawk screech.
When I walk in the woods, I see the deer.
They have lots of fear.
I hear the stream trickle.
The wind through my hair gives me a tickle.
Today there are blue skies.
Grandma is baking delicious cherry pies.

Ashley A. Appleton
Age: 12

MUSHROOMS

I like to go mushroom hunting,
We wrap up in bunting,
Into the woods we go,
We find many! Ho, ho, ho!

Ondra Berglan Shafer
Age: 7

FALL IS HERE!!

Fall is nice, fall is noisy.
Fall is very, very windy.
The leaves start to crunch.
The bluebirds sing.
I like fall because it is cute.

Alyssa Williams
Age: 7

VISIT ME

"Boo hoo," I'm crying for you,
I'm blue without you,
Come visit me,
And you will see!

Matt Huffman
Age: 7

CARROTS

The ferrets ate my carrots,
That has no merits,
I thought that he would eat the rats,
I'm glad he didn't eat the cats!

Andrew Mohler
Age: 8

THE ACCIDENT

There once was a boy
who had a toy,
he fell down the stairs
and broke the chairs!

Susan Alva
Age: 7

THE FOOL CHICKEN

A chicken jumped into a pool
And caught a fool,
His boot caught a mule.
He broke a rule
Oh! How cruel!

Drew Eck
Age: 7

MY NEEDLER FAMILY

Needlers
Are hairy,
Are good runners,
Are nice stubborn people,
Short!

Joshua R. Needler
Age: 10

EVAN

Evan
Short, thin,
Good at school,
Likes to play ball,
Freckles.

Evan Pence
Age: 8

I VENTURED UNDER MY DESK ONE DAY

I ventured under my desk one day,
To get my pencil lead,
I ventured under my desk one day,
I found something else instead.

I ventured under my desk one day,
Something else was there,
I ventured under my desk one day,
With great big eyes and horrible, horrible hair.

I ventured under my desk one day,
With six inch long toes,
I ventured under my desk one day,
With a huge long nose.

I ventured under my desk one day,
He was nine feet tall,
I ventured under my desk one day,
He was not very nice at all.

I ventured under my desk one day,
He was pretty fat,
I ventured under my desk one day,
Now what do you think of that?

I ventured under my desk one day,
His back was pretty bent,
I ventured under my desk one day,
Away I wanted him sent.

I ventured under my desk one day,
He was mean, you know,
I ventured under my desk one day,
I was scared of him so.

Tim Sutherland
Age: 10

JAMIE

Jamie,
Can run,
Fast, I can,
Get along with other
People.

Jamie Marie Bockmon
Age: 9

MARCUS

Marcus
Good, fun,
Good at sports,
Is in third grade,
Nice.

Marcus Corn
Age: 9

MY SHADOW

My shadow follows me
Wherever I am it will be.
When I awake, it doesn't sleep.
Sometimes my shadow
Gives me the creeps!

My shadow rarely goes away.
Sometimes it goes on a rainy day.
Why can't my shadow stay
   that way!

Betheney Ellcessor
Age: 10

GREAT YELLOWSTONE

A poem for two voices

Fires!   Fires!
Black
                 dusty,
smoke
Fires!

In 1988

Fires!   Fires!
of
                 Great
Yellowstone.

Michael Kastner

FOREST FIRE -- 1988

There was a very beautiful land called Yellowstone.
Animals and herds roamed and played.
Rivers, streams and lakes with trees
Hilly land, that day at noon it grew dark,
That night, a very cold and rainy night.
Lightning cracked and fire struck.
Animals hid.
People ran.
Firemen could not stop it.
Planes dumped water.
One day snow fell.
Fire smothered.
Old Faithful blows at 3:00,
Now new life grows.

Travis Schuler

THE VACUUM CLEANER

A giant vacuum sucked me in, just the other day,
The little man inside said "to get out, you have to pay!"
"A quarter and a piece of fuzz. A feather and a dime."
"And an itty bitty spider web, within ten minutes time."
"Ten minutes is all. Not a second later."
If one thing was wrong, I'd be food for alligator.
I had to hurry, Golly Gosh!
I had no time for tish tosh.
Nine minutes left, and I was running,
To find what I need, I sure was hunting.
Eight left now, and all I'd found,
Was the spider web; am I gator bound?
Seven, six, and now five,
I had the quarter, I'm still alive.
Four now three, my feather and dime.
Then the fuzz. I still have time.
Run. Run. Don't trip on that moss!
Hurry up--OH NO! I think I'm lost.
"Run toward the light:" I'd always heard.
So I did, then flew like a bird.
With one second left, I shot out from the vacuum
By that little man. All I could do was say
        THANK YOU!

Christine M. Barger
Age: 15

LIFE IS EVERYTHING

Life is everything
From things in space
To things in a meadow
Life is everything
Everything small
Everything tall
Life is everything
No matter what it is
Life is it
LIFE IS EVERYTHING

Gregory Wilson

Without a tree where would I be.
There would be no houses.
There would be no books.
There would be no gum.
There would be no shade.
There would be no money.
There would be no woods.

Ross Kidd
Age: 8

KRIS

Kris,
Very smart,
I am intelligent,
A very good athlete,
Runner.

Kristopher C. Bright
Age: 9

THE COOL DRAGON

I saw a dragon in a pool.
He used a tool to fix the pool.
The dragon said, "Cool"
The dragon was cool
Because he went to school!

Angela Sage
Age: 8

THE SUN

Golden
Bright shining rays
Beautiful graceful glowing
Handsome regal perfect
The sun

Cory Norman
Age: 10

THE FIRST SPRING DAY

A songbird on your windowsill beckoning for you
to come out.

The wind calling to you "Come on out and play."

The sun's shining and persuading gets you out of
the bed and out the door.

This is how the morning of the first spring day
started.

A soft gentle breeze playfully flutters past
your shoulder.

The soft smell of fresh new pine needles fills
the air with the sweet aroma.

The petals of the flowers bright and metallic,
look crystal-like beneath the sunshine and dew.

Beautiful little flowers along the path,
whisper "Spring is here! Spring is here!"

Afternoon comes and goes with the sunshine at
full force.

Dusk has arrived sending animals into their
burrows, nests, and other homes.

The sun is going down sending out bright,
radiant colors that fill up the sky, like fireworks.

And that is how the first spring day ended.

Emily Bailey
Age: 11

When you read a book,
Your mind is faraway,
Your mind will cook a new idea,
And in your hands the book will stay.

Reading is an adventure,
When you get the right book,
It will take you faraway,
It will give your day a brand new look.

Your mind will grow,
Your heart will soar,
As you turn each page,
You will hunger for some more.

Chapter after chapter,
Until you are done,
Then you'll look back and say,
"That was so much fun!"

Jessica Dyke
Age: 11

A KITCHEN TABLE

My face is round,
my legs are stout.

My once shiny finish is now worn out.
Though I am of many years, I've watched a family grow

from day to day, through many years,
laughter and tears.

Warm meals have been put upon me,
they've shared me with many friends and guests.

I've hardly had time to rest.
Countless excited hellos and tearful good-byes.

The warm sweet smell of cookies and pies.
I silently wait to see them leave and return at the end
   of the day.

I am glad to listen to their problems and
hear them pray.

I'm so happy to be here with the family
for with love they will repay.

Amanda Coleman
Age: 15

WHAT IS LOVE?

Love is a mystery.
It goes back in history.

Love is better than ice cream.
Is it like a daydream.

What is love?
Is it a dove?

What does it mean?
Can it be seen?

Love is a wonderful thing.
It is better than a diamond ring.

It may hurt for a little while.
But soon after, you will start to smile.

Amber O'Bryan
Age: 11

THE FLICKERING CANDLE

Look at that candle sitting by the tree,
Just flickering and looking at me.
Boy, it looks as hot as can be,
A light blue flame just flickering at me.
I wonder if it can bite sitting by the tree.
So, I went over and touched it,
Out of curiosity.
And, Oh Boy, it has teeth!
So I went crying to my mommy and daddy,
And they killed that thing by simply blowing on it.

Zachary Gennicks
Age: 11

THE MIGHTY WARSHIP

Aboard the mighty warship,
On the endless ocean,
Beneath the crashing waves,
Off the coast of the war-stricken island.

Below the waves she lies,
At her berth, she sits,
Inside lie the fallen crewmen,
Throughout her once gleaming hall, they lie.

Since the ship sunk on that stormy night,
On that day, men see her afloat,
But the ship is not afloat,
For it's underneath the waves.

Patrick Dale Howell Knight
Age: 11

BLOOM

It came out of the ground
With the bird's sweet sound.
It started as a seed
but now it is a weed.
It bloomed at night
With the beautiful color white.
It's protected by a rock
With its white colorful chalk.
It gets all nice and dry
When it stretches to the sky.
Now it's full of life
Maybe it can get a wife!

Marc Pate
Age: 12

AUTUMN

Animals playing and getting food,
Under leaves, kids playing
Trees having new, colored leaves
Up the trees, busy squirrels chattering
Mom making pumpkin pies
Nuts falling everywhere

Lisa Kleindorfer
Age: 10

I WOULD LIKE TO BE A BUTTERFLY

I would like to be a butterfly,
With colors on my wings,
To go above the mountaintops,
And hear the angels sing.

I would like to be a butterfly,
I'd fly most everywhere,
Looking at the tall sky,
I'd do somersaults in the air.

Rachel Mallory
Age: 6

YELLOW AS....

Leaves in the fall on the trees.
As butter we put on corn is.
We were looking at the sun, moon, and stars
While we were eating popcorn.
How yellow they are.
   I shouted...
There's a cheetah chasing a bird.
To my sister when she spit out her yellow bread.
   I was drinking...
Lemonade with a lemon on the side.
While I was eating the yolk in an egg.
I saw a daffodil and dandelion.
Chlorophyll giving its yellow color.
   Then my yellow bus went by,
When I was eating French fries and cheese.
That's the end of my yellow history.
Then I started climbing a tree with honey and bees.

Katie Phillips
Age: 10

There was a skeleton named Jim
He noticed he was very slim
He didn't grin
He ate with all his friends
And never came back again

Allie Peters
Age: 11

A FLOWER

I look,
I see
Something prettier than you and me.
What could it be?
A flower!

Samantha Sims
Age: 9

There once was ghost named Scary
His friend was a tiny little fairy
The fairy was named Hi
He always said "Good-bye"
Then they went to see a Canary.

Jeffery D. Birchfield
Age: 11

BILL

There once was a skeleton named Bill.
But he was really still.
Because he was really ill.
So he had to take a pill.
His pill was really a thrill.

Joshua Stevens
Age: 11

THE BIRD

One day a bird came.
She made her nest for her eggs.
Her eggs were spotted.

Amanda Lowe
Age: 10

DADS

Dads are fine
and they don't mind
when you eat
with your mouth full of meat
dads are kind.

Tyler Grace
Age: 11

ELEPHANT SCHOOL

The elephant went to school
And he said, "I'm very cool,"
I learn to read
And count my beads.

Brandi Hicks
Age: 7

Grades
Report cards
A's are best
B's are very good
C's are satisfactory
the rest
downhill

Shera Dixon
Age: 10

THE LOST DOG

I went to the dark park,
And I heard a loud bark.
I noticed that it was Otis.
I didn't call the police.

Jimmie Jackson
Age: 8

SLAM DUNK

There was a skunk.
Who really stunk.
Then one day
He made a slam dunk.
Now no one
Will call him a punk!

Kevin Duncan
Age: 7

SCHOOL DAYS WITH TURKEY

The turkey went to school,
Then he went to the pool
And he rode a mule,
Before he fell into the pool.

Sheldon Sutton, Jr.
Age: 7

WHAT A DAY!

The boat went over the float.
The goat got a boat.
The tool chased the mule.
The cool mule had a stool.
The fool had a duel!
The boy said, "What a day!"

Tyler Deaton
Age: 8

SNAKES

Snakes have beady eyes,
Snakes are different sizes,
Snakes are very neat.

Kelsey Toy
Age: 10

THE HEAD SHRINKER

Once there was a stinker
Who didn't use his thinker
He's called the "Head Shrinker."
Driving to the blinker
He ran into a clinker,
That ends the "Head Shrinker!"

Mark T. Riner
Age: 8

The little rabbit
It is furry and white
A pretty cute pet

Katie Sutter
Age: 10

THE THANKSGIVING TURKEY

There was a turkey
Who was so perky.
Then he got jerky
Also he got worky.
Now he is a perky,
Jerky, worky, lurky
  turkey.

                                        Adam Weaver

Small little bunnies
Hopping in the big green field
Cute little bunnies

                        Nicholas Richard Kellerman
                        Age: 10

EAGLES

Eagles, eagles in the sky.
Gee, they really love to fly.

Way up to the mountaintops.
The eagles never want to stop.

They spread their wings out so wide,
They use them as a guide.

Kyle Mohler
Age: 8

Football
Hard hitting and rough
Pass blocking gang tackling
Grass eating touchdown running sport
Helmet cracking game

Kyle Louis Combs
Age: 10

FALL IS FINALLY HERE

The birds fly south.
There are hundred's
of leaves on the ground.
The trees are dying
the leaves are falling.
The trees are dry.

Kevin Manley
Age: 8

THE SUN SHINING BRIGHT

I like sun a lot
especially when it's bright
I think that it's neat

Todd Matthew Rosenberger
Age: 9

KITTENS

Kittens, kittens, I love kittens,
Kittens so playful, so soft.
Kittens, kittens, I love kittens.
Want some kittens, I do.

Amanda Peters
Age: 10

TRAPS

Traps, traps,
They're all around.
If you see one,
Get out of town!

Juliette van Gils
Age: 6

AUTUMN

Autumn
Tall, trim, and nice.
Loves the sun and deer too.
Loves to read about mysteries.
Special.

Autumn Wagner
Age: 8

Stars are very bright!
The sun is a big star!
At night and day you can see the sun!
Right after the sun is gone the other stars come out.
Sometimes stars don't come out at night.

Amanda Fritsch
Age: 9

STARS

Stars,
Tiny, bright,
Beautiful little lights,
Dancing in the sky,
Stars.

Danielle Wagoner
Age: 10

Thanksgiving
fun, delicious
loving, giving, sharing
is for giving thanks
Holiday

Melissa Mauch
Age: 9

LIGHT

Waiting...
Waiting to break free,
Break free from all the soundless
Darkness and sorrow away,
Faraway.

Tabitha Smith

THE AMANDA PANDA BEAR

My name's Amanda,
I am a Panda.
I am black and white,
I sleep real tight.
I chase the bugs way away,
Then I say, "Okay!"

Amanda Bright
Age: 8

BASKETBALL

I
Love the
Feeling of metal
Smacking on my hand
Slam dunk

Jason Prater
Age: 10

FOREVER FREE

And so it is,
that they may fly off on their velvet wings,
or so on their wings of gold,
to a field,
where they,
and only the truth,
can be forever free.

Jamie Nicley
Age: 12

SPRING

Spring,
Flowers are growing.
Hot weather is coming.
Butterflies flying in the air.
Flying, hot, growing.

Melanie Kuns
Age: 10

THE ZOMBIE

In the dark graveyard,
Under the lifeless tree,
Near the mangled tombstone,
Behind me, arises a zombie.

Across the graveyard, running for my life,
Without a doubt,
Toward my house,
Against the fence, I am relieved.

Stephanie Phegley
Age: 12

PRESENT

There is a present by the wall,
It looks so fat and tall,
It is the best of all,
But it wasn't for me at all.

Rachel Sims
Age: 11

The month of November is cold
The wind can blow hard, I'm told
The leaves turn from green
To the prettiest colors you've ever seen
Now you know that time has grown old

Amber Seger
Age: 6

LOVE LASTS

Love will still be yours,
a gift from me to you,
through gloomy days,
and sunshine rays,
Love will still be yours!

For Daddy and Mommy
who made childhood beautiful.

Kelsey Warren
Age: 7

BASEBALL

Ryan,
Good ballplayer,
Very good hitter,
He can field well,
Athletic.

Ryan Worrel
Age: 9

HEAVEN

I think of Heaven in a really big cloud,
Safe and not so very loud.
You think of Heaven as a great big castle,
Where there's not much of a hassle.
Though we think of Heaven in both a different way,
We'll both go to Heaven, somehow, someday.

Emily Rose Wenrich

THINGS THAT ARE RED

Red is hot.
Red is the color of a flag.
An apple is red,
A fire truck is red,
Clothes are red,
Christmas bells are red.
All things are red,
But I can't name all things
That are red.

Samantha Cline
Age: 7

WHITNEY

My name's Whitney Worrel.
I'm an eight year old girl.
I have a pretty cat.
Her name is Shirt.

I like to play dolls.
I don't often throw balls.
I love to read a book.
And to help my mom cook.

Whitney Worrel
Age: 8

THE JET PET

I have a pet
His name is Jet,
Because I met him
In a jet
My pet is a jet pet!
Can you believe
He did not have a vet?

Laura Ann Hutchison
Age: 7

ABOUT ME

I go outside to play with the cats,
I also play with the dog.

I play at the park sometimes and it is fun.
Sometimes I play inside too.

Madeline Overman
Age: 8

SPORTS

Sarah,
plays basketball,
good at it,
likes going bike riding,
Athletic.

Sarah Lewis
Age: 8